CW01512617

Original title:
Wistful Fissures Among the Wizard Rail

Author: Olivia Oja
ISBN HARDBACK: 978-1-80559-487-1
ISBN PAPERBACK: 978-1-80559-986-9

Fables from the Arcane Railway

Whispers ride the ancient tracks,
Beneath the moonlit sky so black.
Dreams entwined with smoke and steam,
Fables born from a midnight dream.

Mystic stories float in air,
Charming all who stop and stare.
Each station holds a hidden tale,
Of magic lost on a spectral trail.

Guardians of the rails now rest,
Each ghost a memory possessed.
The rhythm of the night's embrace,
Further drives this dreamy chase.

With lanterns lit in twilight's hue,
They beckon souls, both old and new.
Their laughter echoes through the night,
A tapestry of dark and light.

Fables spun like threads of gold,
In every heart, a story told.
The trains roll on, unseen, unknown,
In every whisper, magic's sewn.

The Silent Song of Wandering Wizards

In twilight's glow, the wizards roam,
With quiet spells, they find their home.
In shadows deep, their secrets weave,
A silent song that few believe.

Through moons of silver, they take flight,
Crafting realms beyond our sight.
Their laughter soft, like drifting leaves,
In every note, a magic breathes.

Time unfurls as they dance and glide,
Over hills, where dreams abide.
Their wisdom flows like crystal streams,
In every glance, a world of dreams.

Yet silence wraps their paths in mist,
In every shadowed turn, a twist.
With fleeting forms, they faze away,
A whispered spell, an unseen play.

For in their hearts, a heavy tune,
Bound by stars, beneath the moon.
The silent song will never fade,
A magic born from twilight's shade.

Illusions in the Flickering Dusk

In the dusk's embrace, illusions bloom,
Casting shadows, weaving gloom.
Colors clash in twilight's dance,
Each flicker pulls you in a trance.

Mirrors lie upon the ground,
Reflecting whispers, no sound.
In this realm, what's real will bend,
Truth and fabrications blend.

Figures shimmer, then dissolve,
Mysteries that the night involves.
With every step, the pathway sways,
Lost in this haze of twilight rays.

Fantasies diverging like streams,
Crafting tales from fleeting dreams.
In the heartbeat of the night,
Illusions dance just out of sight.

But wanderers, heed the dusk's refrain,
In every joy, there's hidden pain.
Through flickering flames, we seek the true,
Yet find ourselves forever blue.

Fragmented Memories on the Sorcerous Track

On sorcerous tracks of broken dreams,
Whispers echo in silent schemes.
Memories scattered in the night,
Lost between wrong and right.

With each step, the past unfolds,
Tales of love, of courage bold.
Haunting faces flash and fade,
In the twilight's soft parade.

Fragments glint like shattered glass,
Moments passed that cannot last.
Every heartbeat carries forth,
The weight of dreams, the burden's worth.

Upon this track, the heart will race,
Chasing shadows, seeking grace.
In dreams and echoes, wisdom grows,
As through the night, the spirit flows.

Yet as the dawn begins to creep,
We gather memories, theirs to keep.
In every crack, a story lies,
Fragmented truth behind the skies.

Haikus of the Wandering Mage

Footsteps on soft ground,
Whispers of ancient spells,
Stars guide the lost heart,
Winds carry secrets far.

In shadows, a flicker,
A lantern's gentle glow,
Paths woven in starlight,
Echoes of spellbound dreams.

With each step, a story,
A journey through the night,
Nature's vibrant dance calls,
Magic in every breath.

Clouds drift like memories,
Mountains cradle the sky,
Time slips through one's fingers,
The mage continues on.

In the heart's deep silence,
Wisdom flows like rivers,
A song of longing plays,
The wanderer seeks peace.

The Enchanted Station of Lost Paths

Beneath the old oak,
Tracks of time intertwine,
Whispers in the breeze,
Magic lives in the air.

Candles flicker softly,
Shadows dance on the walls,
Memories take their form,
Guiding lost souls back home.

The clock ticks with purpose,
Moments fly like paper,
Lost paths fade from the day,
Yet linger in the dream.

A train of thoughts departs,
Carrying faded hopes,
Each stop a chance to learn,
What once was, can return.

Embrace the magic here,
Every choice shapes the way,
In the heart of the night,
A new path reveals light.

Spirit Trails Through the Night

Footfalls on the ground,
Guiding spirits around,
Moonlight paints the path,
Echoes of those who roam.

Stars shimmer like whispers,
Hints of tales untold,
Winds carry soft secrets,
Among the silver leaves.

Souls drift in shadows,
Their stories intertwined,
Restless in the twilight,
Seeking peace in the dark.

A lantern in my hand,
Casts warmth through the chill,
Following the old trails,
Where memories reside.

Together on this journey,
We dance amid the night,
Life's tapestry unfolds,
In the glow of lost dreams.

A Soliloquy for Forgotten Entrances

In the quiet corners,
Where echoes softly fade,
Lost doors guard secrets,
Whispered tales of the past.

Each entrance beckons me,
With promises of change,
The weight of forgotten,
Hangs heavy in the air.

I tread on gentle paths,
With memories in tow,
A heart full of longing,
For the doors left ajar.

Time wraps around my heart,
In places once alive,
A dance of shadows swirls,
Through portals to the light.

So here I stand alone,
In the glow of lost dreams,
A soliloquy sings,
For entrances unseen.

The Longing of an Arcane Heart

In shadows deep, the secrets lie,
A whisper soft, a distant sigh.
Stars above, they twinkle bright,
Yet in my chest, an endless night.

Ancient spells, they weave and spin,
Each heartbeat sings of love within.
But magic lost, a fleeting grace,
Leaves but a trace, a hollow space.

Forgotten dreams in silence weep,
For all the promises we keep.
A flicker dims, its glow confined,
Yet hope still lingers, undefined.

With every pulse, the echoes call,
A dance of shadows on the wall.
I reach for stars with trembling hands,
Yet find myself in barren lands.

Oh, arcane heart, set free your flame,
For every longing, every name.
Through the abyss, let courage steer,
And break the chains that bind me here.

Journey Through Shattered Reflections

Mirrors crack, the truth revealed,
A path forgotten, fate concealed.
Each shard reflects a piece of me,
In fragments lost, I yearn to see.

Steps uncertain on jagged glass,
Where memories whisper, then swiftly pass.
Haunted faces, familiar yet strange,
A dance of life, a haunting change.

Through the haze, a lantern glows,
Guiding the way where darkness flows.
Every tear, a glimmer bright,
Shattering shadows with hopeful light.

In every crack, a story lies,
Of love and loss, of whispered goodbyes.
With courage found in fragile streams,
I journey forth through broken dreams.

The road ahead, though lined with fears,
Will lead me past the weight of years.
And as I walk, I'll find my way,
To brighter dawns and new bouquet.

Glimmers of Magic in Fleeting Dreams

In twilight's grasp, dreams weave and sway,
Softly whispering of worlds at play.
Each shimmer dances on night's embrace,
A fleeting spark in time and space.

Moonlit paths and stardust trails,
Where fantasy blooms and courage sails.
Every shadow holds secrets near,
Glimmers of magic, washed in cheer.

With every breath, the dreams ignite,
Painting visions in silver light.
Hope, the canvas, and joy, the brush,
Creating wonders in the hush.

Through dreams we chase, the heart's delight,
In whispered tales of endless night.
The ephemeral dance of wishes spun,
In magic's cradle, we are one.

Hold tight the visions, let them soar,
For in this magic, we yearn for more.
Each dream, a promise, a guiding star,
Leading us onward, no matter how far.

The Enchanted Departure

When twilight falls, the world departs,
A hush descends, entwined with hearts.
Beneath the glow of ancient trees,
Whispers carried on the breeze.

With every step, the magic thrums,
A symphony of distant drums.
The path unfolds, a tale untold,
In every echo, adventure bold.

Farewell to those we hold so dear,
The journey calls, we must not fear.
Though parting aches, we must believe,
In every end, a chance to weave.

The stars align, their light divine,
As fate entwines with yours and mine.
A tapestry of dreams, so grand,
We step together, hand in hand.

At dawn's first light, our spirits soar,
In every heartbeat, we'll explore.
This enchanted night, where hope ignites,
Marks the departure to new heights.

Lanterns Along the Mystic Path

Softly glowing lanterns dance,
Casting whispers on the ground.
They guide the steps of dreams,
Where secrets can be found.

In twilight's gentle embrace,
Shadows weave a tender tale.
Each flicker sparks a memory,
As night begins to pale.

A pathway kissed by moonlight,
Where wishes dare to roam.
The lanterns, like protectors,
Lead us safely home.

With each step, a heartbeat shared,
Echoes of the past reside.
Together in this mystic glow,
We cast the dark aside.

Lanterns bobbing in the night,
Each a story yet untold.
They call to those who wander,
With hearts both brave and bold.

Murmurs of the Enchanted Passage

In shadows deep, the murmurs rise,
Whispers of a hidden lore.
The passage glimmers, drawing near,
An adventure to explore.

A gentle breeze unveils the path,
As petals flutter to the ground.
Every footstep echoes softly,
With secrets all around.

Voices of the ancients call,
In melodies of long ago.
They guide our hearts through tangled woods,
To places few may know.

Each turn reveals a tale anew,
As daylight starts to fade.
Within this enchanted passage,
Our destinies are made.

As twilight deepens all around,
The stars awake and gleam.
In silence, we embrace the night,
And awaken from the dream.

Shattered Realities of Wandering Souls

In a world of broken mirrors,
Where reflections seem to fade.
Wandering souls search for the truth,
In the games that fate has played.

Each fragment tells a story lost,
Of times they could have been.
A tapestry of choices made,
With paths they never seen.

Ghostly echoes haunt the air,
In this realm of what has passed.
They whisper of the lives undone,
And future shadows cast.

Through the shattered veil we roam,
In search of brighter days.
Yet still, the past lingers on,
Like distant, smoky haze.

But hope remains a flickering light,
In the dance of fate's embrace.
Wandering souls find solace here,
In this ethereal space.

Fantasies on the Edge of a Spellbound Journey

At the edge of dreams and dawn,
Fantasies begin to rise.
Each step a dance of wonder,
Beneath enchanted skies.

Woven tales of magic spun,
Like silk upon the breeze.
They draw the brave to venture forth,
Unraveling with ease.

With hearts aflame and spirits high,
We leap into the unknown.
Each moment, a resplendent breath,
In realms where dreams are sown.

As laughter twirls on silver threads,
And stardust fills the air.
We forge our paths through twilight's glow,
Together without care.

A spellbound journey waits ahead,
With wonders yet to see.
In this dance of fantasy,
We find our spirits free.

Cracks in the Realm of Fantasia

In shadows deep where wonders wait,
A whisper calls through silent gates.
With colors bright that softly soar,
We dance along a dreamlike shore.

Beneath the sky of vibrant hues,
The echoes weave their ancient blues.
Each star that twinkles, bright and grand,
Holds secrets of this timeless land.

Through tangled woods where fairies play,
The twilight lingers, turning gray.
In every shift of breeze and light,
A joy ignites the endless night.

Yet cracks appear in dreams we chase,
As doubts intrude, they leave a trace.
We wander lost, yet still believe,
That in the dark, we may perceive.

So hold my hand, let's venture near,
To realms where fantasy draws near.
With hearts entwined, we'll face the fear,
For in this place, our dreams are clear.

Reverie Beneath the Mystic Arch

Beneath the arch of stars we sigh,
In mirrored dreams where shadows lie.
A soft glow wraps the silent air,
In peace we drift without a care.

Each breath a melody of night,
Awakens hopes and sparks of light.
The moonlight dances on the stream,
A gentle touch of every dream.

Through whispers sweet, the past returns,
With every heart, a passion burns.
In this embrace of cosmic chance,
We find our fate, we find our dance.

Yet as we bow to time's embrace,
We chase the lines, we trace the space.
With every heartbeat, echoing,
We tread the path of remembering.

In reverie, our spirits soar,
As endless tales forever pour.
In harmony, we claim our part,
Each echo sings within the heart.

Fragments of a Celestial Journey

From starlit trails where wishes roam,
We gather light to call us home.
Each fragment casts a golden thread,
In pathways where the brave have tread.

With cosmic dust, our dreams are spun,
In galaxies where hearts are one.
Together we embark on flights,
Through endless realms of endless nights.

A tapestry of fate unfolds,
With whispers of the brave and bold.
Each heartbeat echoes through the spheres,
In vibrant notes that calm our fears.

Yet as we soar on wings of chance,
The shadows urge a fleeting glance.
We hold the stars, we claim the night,
And in that grasp, we find the light.

As fragments dance, our tales ignite,
Across the sky, we chase the bright.
In unity, we find our way,
Through cosmic realms, forever stay.

A Tapestry of Twilight's Secrets

In twilight's glow, the secrets weave,
A tapestry of dreams conceive.
With every thread, a story spins,
In whispered tones, the night begins.

The colors blend, dusk paints the air,
With hints of magic everywhere.
Among the stars, we find our fate,
In every choice, we elevate.

With shadows soft that cradle grace,
We chase the light, we find our place.
In every sigh, a promise made,
In every heartbeat, dreams cascade.

Yet twilight holds its mysteries,
In every sigh, our histories.
As night enfolds, we seek to know,
The secrets in the stars that glow.

So take my hand, let's brave the dusk,
With heartbeats strong and love's bold trust.
In twilight's arms, our journey starts,
A tapestry born from our hearts.

Echoes of Enchantment

In the glade where secrets dwell,
Mysteries weave a timeless spell.
Gentle breezes dance and play,
Guiding lost souls on their way.

Moonlit shadows softly brush,
Hearts awaken in the hush.
Every whisper calls them near,
Chasing dreams that disappear.

Dancing lights in twilight's glow,
Guide the wanderers below.
Among the trees, they find their truth,
In echoes of forgotten youth.

Through the mist, the fairies sigh,
Carrying tales that never die.
With every step, the magic flows,
In this world where wonder grows.

Time stands still, the night is kind,
Leaving all the doubts behind.
In this realm, the heart takes flight,
Echoing in the soft moonlight.

Shadows in the Midnight Grove

Beneath the boughs where whispers sigh,
Shadows linger, passing by.
Silent watchers in the night,
Guard the dreams that take to flight.

Stars above weave silver lace,
Guiding souls to find their place.
In the hush, the spirits speak,
Of lost love and futures bleak.

Rustling leaves tell ancient tales,
Of secret hunts and whispered trails.
In the dark, a soft light glows,
Illuminating where hope grows.

Echoes paint the air with sighs,
Mingling truth with painted lies.
In the grove where shadows roam,
Hearts awaken, finding home.

Moonlit paths of silver shine,
Drawing souls to intertwine.
In this grove, fears take their flight,
As shadows dance in soft moonlight.

Whispers of Forgotten Spells

In the quiet of the night,
Whispers weave with pure delight.
Casting spells of joy and pain,
Binding hearts with gentle chains.

Ancient words upon the breeze,
Stirring memories with such ease.
Every thought like rippling streams,
Flowing through the fractured dreams.

From the depths, lost echoes rise,
Telling truths in veiled disguise.
Once forgotten, now they gleam,
Revealing shadows of a dream.

In the dusk, the past will call,
Drifting softly, over all.
With each murmur in the night,
The forgotten finds the light.

In that moment, magic stirs,
In the heart, an answer purrs.
Though shadows linger, fears compel,
Embrace the whispers, cast the spell.

The Broken Path of Starry Dreams

On a night where wishes break,
Travelers walk with hearts at stake.
Stars above, a fractured glow,
Guide the paths of those who know.

Through the silence, dreams take form,
In the quiet, hope grows warm.
Each step forward, shadows cling,
Yet the heart learns how to sing.

Beneath the weight of fleeting time,
Glistening moments softly chime.
Chasing dawn with bated breath,
Finding life within the death.

Fragments lost, but not in vain,
Each scar a mark where love was slain.
Yet from these ruins, dreams will rise,
Painting colors in the skies.

In the distance, a whisper calls,
Echoing through forgotten halls.
The path ahead may twist and bend,
But starry dreams shall never end.

Shadows Dancing on the Celestial Track

In the stillness of night,
Shadows spin and sway.
Whispers of stars collide,
Carving paths to stray.

Moonlight spills like silk,
Glimmers on the ground.
Each flicker tells a tale,
Of the lost and found.

A dance of ancient lore,
Beneath the cosmic breath.
Every step a memory,
Born of life and death.

Galaxies twirl above,
Their secrets intertwined.
In the velvet darkness,
New horizons find.

While time drifts like a mist,
The shadows play their part.
Guiding lost wanderers,
With a flickering heart.

The Sorcerer's Lament at Dusk

As twilight casts its spell,
The sorcerer stands lone.
With a heart heavy and dark,
He conjures dreams of stone.

Echoes of missed chances,
Whisper through the air.
Incantations of the past,
Fill the night with care.

His wand, a crooked staff,
Bears the weight of dread.
Bringing forth the shadows,
Of the things he said.

With each flick of his wrist,
He yearns for what was lost.
But time is a cruel master,
And he pays the cost.

Though magic fills the dusk,
His spirit fades away.
In the loneliness of night,
He mourns the light of day.

Fleeting Steps of a Dream Weaver

In the garden of the night,
Where dreams whisper and sigh.
A weaver twirls the threads,
Underneath a starry sky.

Her fingers dance with grace,
Stitching visions in the air.
Each strand a glimpse of worlds,
With a delicate care.

But dreams like dew drop fast,
Fleeting in their embrace.
The weaver's heart beats wild,
In this ephemeral space.

Yet as dawn's light approaches,
Her tapestry starts to fray.
She smiles at what was spun,
As night gives way to day.

The echoes of her work,
Fade as the sun begins.
But in the heart of those,
The dream forever spins.

Corners of Infinity between Dreams and Reality

In corners dark and deep,
Where dreams and truths collide.
A realm of fleeting thoughts,
Where all fears must abide.

The veil is thin and worn,
Twisting in the light.
As hopes and fears entwine,
In the loom of night.

Time bends and intertwines,
In this mystical space.
Where the whispers of the past,
Bring shadows to the chase.

With each breath drawn anew,
The edges softly blur.
Reality melts away,
Into the dreamer's purr.

Yet here in this still place,
We dance on time's own string.
Between the breaths of life,
The infinite takes wing.

Chasing Shadows on the Arcane Trail

Through the mist, whispers play,
Faint glimmers of light stray.
Footsteps dance on winding paths,
Secrets held in nature's baths.

Beneath the boughs, shadows creep,
Ancient tales that silence keep.
Echoes of the past arise,
From the depths of twilight skies.

With every turn, a riddle speaks,
A haunting grace the silence seeks.
Silhouettes in moonlit haze,
Guide the heart through winding ways.

In the twilight, dreams unfold,
Stories woven, truths retold.
Chasing visions, breathless chase,
Captured in this mystic space.

As night embraces all around,
In shadows' grip, the truth is found.
On this trail, forever roam,
The arcane whispers lead us home.

An Echo of Illumined Dreams

In the quiet of the night,
Dreams emerge, glowing bright.
Canvas painted with desire,
Hearts ignited, souls on fire.

Whispers from the stars descend,
Every thought, another bend.
Illuminated paths we trace,
Guided by a cosmic grace.

Mirrors reflecting hidden hues,
In the dark, the heart renews.
Each echo a promise kept,
A gentle way for love to step.

Caught between the seams of time,
Voices chant in rhythmic rhyme.
As memories drift on a beam,
Together, we chase the dream.

In this realm of shimmering light,
The shadows melt into the night.
An echo of what's yet to be,
Illumined by our destiny.

When Stars Collide with Wandering Thoughts

When stars collide, a spark ignites,
Illusions dance in endless nights.
Thoughts like comets streak and sway,
Lost in the cosmos' grand ballet.

In the silence, echoes rise,
Wandering dreams in distant skies.
Each twinkle holds a fleeting glance,
A chance to join fate's wild dance.

Weaving through the fabric of time,
Rhythmic pulses, feelings climb.
Galaxies spin, entwined, and astir,
Thoughts collide, hearts start to blur.

In this vastness, we're alone,
Yet the universe calls us home.
In the chaos, find your peace,
When thoughts collide, they never cease.

Carried on the starlit breeze,
Wandering thoughts become the keys.
Unlock the night with dreams so bold,
When stars collide, the magic unfolds.

The Enigma of the Twilight Train

Underneath a sky of gray,
Whispers ride the twilight train.
Journeying through dark and light,
In this realm where shadows bite.

Passengers in silent thought,
With heavy hearts, each bears a lot.
The whistle blows, a haunting call,
Secrets beckon from the hall.

Tracks of memories intertwine,
Fading visions lose their shine.
Yet the heart stays ever still,
Longing for the fleeting thrill.

As shadows stretch and daylight wanes,
The enigma weaves through hidden veins.
Strangers share a fleeting glance,
Bound by fate, they take a chance.

At journeys' end, the truth revealed,
In twilight's grasp, all hearts are healed.
Ride the train through dusk and dawn,
Where enigmas transform and spawn.

The Silken Threads of Wandering Thoughts

In the quiet corners of my mind,
Whispers dance like fragile leaves.
Each thought a thread, soft and fine,
Weaving tapestries that never grieve.

Colors blend in a silent hue,
Patterns shift like restless dreams.
Memories weave a tale so true,
In shadows cast by silver beams.

Threads of joy and threads of woe,
Intertwined in a gentle clutch.
Through winding paths, they ebb and flow,
A fabric soft to hold and touch.

As daylight fades, the tapestry glows,
Illuminating what once was lost.
Each thread a journey, every thread knows,
The price of longing, the weight of cost.

In this dance of thoughts, I roam,
A wanderer with no defined end.
Embracing the chaos, I find my home,
In the silken threads that fate will send.

Tales from the Pendulum's End

Time ticks softly, a gentle chime,
In corners where shadows are cast.
Each swing of the pendulum defines,
The moments that fade and the memories past.

Stories hang in the air, like mist,
Captured in the hands of fate.
Echoes whisper of dreams dismissed,
In chambers where dreams patiently wait.

Fingers reach for what once was gold,
Hope lingers like dust in the light.
Tales of laughter or love untold,
Fleeting shadows escaping the night.

A ticking heart, relentless and bold,
Measures the hours, the years, the way.
In the stillness, secrets unfold,
As the pendulum swings day by day.

At journey's end, we share the fire,
Of stories woven and lives we've spent.
In each heartbeat, we find desire,
In the tales from the pendulum's end.

Echoes Trapped in Starlit Tunnels

In the quiet of the starlit night,
Echoes linger, soft as prayer.
Whispers float like a feather's flight,
Lost in the tunnels of deep despair.

Each star a dream that dared to shine,
Reflections of hopes that never ceased.
In shadows long, the worlds align,
Silent songs of a cosmic feast.

Time unravels in spiral threads,
Connecting us through unseen paths.
In the silence where beauty spreads,
Life and death interlace their wraths.

Beneath the veil of the midnight hue,
Echoes call to those who will hear.
In starlit tunnels, the journey's true,
A symphony played through joy and fear.

Captured moments in a starry embrace,
Unraveled tales of the wild unknown.
In echoes bound, we find our place,
A journey shared, no longer alone.

The Train Whistle of Destiny

A train whistle sings in the cool night air,
Calling forth dreams from the depths of sleep.
Tracks laid down with a careful care,
Each journey taken, a promise to keep.

Through valleys wide and mountains steep,
The train rolls on, a heart so bold.
In every clatter, we laugh and weep,
As stories of destiny gently unfold.

Passengers gaze with hope in their eyes,
Watching landscapes blur and bend.
Chasing horizons beneath endless skies,
With every mile, we write our end.

The locomotive breathes like a living thing,
Pulling forth dreams from the distant past.
In the echo of iron, our spirits sing,
As time drifts by, fleeting and fast.

Onward it goes, this train of fate,
With every whistle, a new breath begins.
Where tracks may lead, we cannot wait,
For destiny waits as our journey spins.

The Lure of Enigmatic Winds

Whispers dance through ancient trees,
A voice carried on the breeze.
Mysteries in every gust,
In twilight's glow, we place our trust.

Clouds swirl in a velvet sky,
Secrets travel, oh so sly.
They beckon us to venture near,
In shadows lurk what we hold dear.

A call beyond the mountain ridge,
Where hidden paths weave like a bridge.
The world shifts with every sigh,
In the winds, our dreams can fly.

A melody, soft and true,
Leads to places known by few.
Each breath a step to realms unknown,
In the winds, we create our own.

So take my hand; let's boldly roam,
In every gust, we'll find our home.
The winds will guide us, hearts alight,
Together, we embrace the night.

Stardust Trails and Lost Tomes

Beneath the stars, the stories glow,
Worn pages hide the tales of old.
Each word a spark, a cosmic thread,
In dreams of starlight, we tread.

Lost are the tomes by time erased,
Yet their essence cannot be chased.
With every glance, a memory glows,
Through stardust trails, our spirit flows.

In hidden chambers of the night,
We seek the truth, igniting light.
A quest for wisdom, pure and rare,
The cosmos whispers in the air.

With ink of moonbeams on our lips,
We journey forth on moonlit ships.
Each chapter woven in the dark,
Illuminates the secrets' spark.

As we explore this vast expanse,
Celestial wonders lead the dance.
In every tome, a universe waits,
Unraveled softly by our fates.

Veins of Magic and Memory

In forests deep, where shadows play,
The veins of magic softly sway.
Through ancient roots, the whispers flow,
A tapestry of tales we sow.

Memory hangs like morning dew,
Glimmers of gold in every hue.
Each moment captured, a breath held tight,
In sacred spaces wrapped in light.

The pulse of time, a gentle tug,
In the silence, a heartstring dug.
Within each leaf, a secret lies,
A world unseen beneath the skies.

Echoes thread through the night air,
Binding earth and sky with care.
In veins of magic, we take flight,
Our souls ignite with pure delight.

So come, my friend, and feel the beat,
A rhythm that makes the world complete.
In every heartbeat, tales reside,
In veins of memory, we confide.

Echoes of the Unwritten

In silence dwells the untold song,
Echoes linger, where dreams belong.
Each page awaits a lover's sigh,
A story yearning to fly high.

Whispers cradle a poet's mind,
In every stroke, worlds entwined.
The beauty of what could have been,
Lives in the spaces, soft and thin.

Ink flows like rivers of time,
Crafting verses, a silent rhyme.
In shadows long, the words take flight,
From the edges of the night.

With hands that tremble, hearts will share,
The burdens of hope, the dreams laid bare.
In echoes, we shall surely find,
The stories lost, the ties that bind.

Let us wander where few have tread,
Through realms of thoughts, where some have fled.
In these echoes, we shall define,
The beauty of the unwritten line.

A Whisp of Starlit Fantasies

In velvet night where dreams ignite,
Starlit whispers dance in flight.
They twine around the daisy's glow,
Embracing tales of long ago.

A sigh escapes the moon's embrace,
As shadows weave a tender grace.
With every gleam, a wish takes form,
In starlit skies where hearts are warm.

The echoes hum of ancient lore,
Beneath the stars, we long for more.
Each shimmering spark, a gentle guide,
Towards the dreams we hold inside.

A canvas blank, the cosmos wide,
Where fantasies and wishes bide.
With every twinkling star so near,
We paint our hopes, our joys, our fear.

So close your eyes and breathe it in,
The starlit tales, where dreams begin.
For in the night, all secrets bloom,
Leaving whispers in the room.

Chimeras on the Ghostly Express

On rails of mist, the phantoms glide,
With echoes soft, they slip and slide.
In twilight's grasp, their forms take flight,
Chimeras dance in fading light.

The whistle blows, a mournful call,
As shadows stretch and softly fall.
Each passenger, a tale untold,
In the spectral coach, where dreams unfold.

The lanterns flicker with ghostly glee,
As memories drift like old sea debris.
With every stop, a story shared,
Of love and loss, of hearts once bared.

They ride through realms where time stands still,
On trains of thoughts that fate may fill.
In whispered tones, the past arrives,
While chimeras dance, the spirit thrives.

So take a seat and ponder deep,
What dreams await as shadows creep.
For on this train, the lost reside,
In chimeras where hopes abide.

The Morning After the Arcane Storm

The dawn breaks clear, the world transformed,
After the night where magic warmed.
With whispers soft from skies anew,
The air is thick with dreams that brew.

Puddles glisten like molten glass,
Reflecting tales of storms that pass.
Fractals dance on emerald leaves,
While sunlight weaves what the heart believes.

The clouds have fled, the sky's a slate,
Where hope arises, where dreams await.
Each breath, a promise fiercely born,
Innocence gleams, the day reborn.

The world awakes, a hush profound,
As new beginnings swirl around.
With every ray that kisses skin,
The morning shines, inviting kin.

So hold this moment, tender, bright,
As shadows yield to warmth and light.
For after storms, the sun must rise,
And paint the world in vibrant skies.

Pathways of Light Lost in Time

Beneath the boughs where silence reigns,
Pathways of light weave through the plains.
Each step evokes a ghostly sight,
As footsteps echo, bold yet light.

The ancient woods hold secrets deep,
Where time drifts slow, and shadows creep.
In golden hues, the dawn unveils,
The whispered paths of forgotten tales.

A flicker glows amidst the trees,
Guiding souls like a gentle breeze.
In twilight's kiss, we find the way,
Through light and shadow, night and day.

With every turn, a tale unfolds,
Of dreams once lost, of hearts so bold.
The pathways twist, both near and far,
Guided by the light of a wandering star.

So wander free, let spirits rise,
On luminous trails beneath the skies.
For in the twilight, hope ignites,
On pathways of light, where love invites.

Shadows Across the Ethereal Plains

Beneath the sky, shadows dance,
Whispers of dreams in a forgotten trance.
Ghostly figures, they sway and glide,
In the stillness, where secrets reside.

Echoes of hope in the twilight haze,
Carried on winds through shadowed ways.
Stars flicker above like lost memories,
Guiding the hearts beneath ancient trees.

Every heartbeat paints the night wide,
Breathing life into the silence implied.
Paths intertwine in a delicate waltz,
Merging the realms, lost in the vaults.

In the whispers of dusk, time is slow,
Unraveling tales only shadows know.
Every flutter of leaves tells a story,
Of faded glories and fleeting glory.

Together they weave through the ether's seam,
In a fragile embrace, entwined in a dream.
Silhouettes linger, softly they sigh,
As shadows across the plains brush the sky.

The Lingering Touch of Unseen Forces

In the silence, a current hums,
A touch of senses as spirit comes.
Threads of fate weave through the air,
Connecting the souls, a hidden affair.

Fingers of light beckon the night,
Unseen forces guide with delight.
Whispers of wisdom float round the space,
Time bends softly in their grace.

Echoing heartbeats like thunderous drums,
Resonating where the mystery comes.
Moments collide in a dance so rare,
Guided by hands of the unseen care.

Shadows weave tales in the twilight glow,
Secrets unravel in the ebb and flow.
Carried on breezes, they softly implore,
To listen closely, to seek and explore.

Each sigh of the wind holds a message,
A tale of connection, a passage,
Through realms unknown, journey we must,
Trusting the touch, we lose and we trust.

Twilight's Unraveled Threads

Twilight descends with a gentle sigh,
Painting the world in colors that lie.
Threads of day slowly intertwine,
With the stars that shimmer like aged wine.

The horizon glows with secrets untold,
In whispers of dusk, the night unfolds.
Every breath a canvas of fleeting light,
Threads unravel, giving way to the night.

Dreams take shape in the velvety dark,
Painting the silence, igniting a spark.
Echoes of laughter linger in the breeze,
As twilight wraps all in a soft tease.

Fingers of shadow draw close to the sun,
As day's final light dares to run.
Each moment a treasure, softly released,
In the dance of twilight, we find our peace.

The night creeps forth, steady and calm,
A symphony played on the world's palm.
In the gentle folds of this quiet domain,
Twilight's threads whisper, never in vain.

Moments Suspended in Time's Gaze

In the stillness, moments freeze,
Caught between breaths, a subtle tease.
A glance exchanged, hearts align,
Time halts briefly, love's divine.

Each heartbeat echoes, softly sings,
Captured within, the joy it brings.
Fragments of laughter caught in the air,
A tapestry woven with precious care.

Shadows of memories play on the wall,
Fleeting reflections, then silence falls.
In the weight of an embrace, worlds collide,
Moments suspended, where dreams abide.

Time's gentle fingers brush past our skin,
Drawing the lines of where we've been.
Every heartbeat a snapshot held dear,
Moments suspended, forever near.

Through the veil of time, we softly tread,
In whispered thoughts, the unmapped thread.
With every sigh, a memory spins,
In the gaze of time, where life begins.

The Dance of the Elusive Spirits

In shadows deep, they twirl and spin,
Whispers lost to the night's soft din.
Glimmers fade where they touch the ground,
Echoes of joy in silence found.

Moonlight weaves through branches high,
Casting dreams where secrets lie.
With every step, the night they grace,
A fleeting glimpse, a ghostly trace.

Their laughter dances on the breeze,
A melody that brings one to their knees.
Elusive forms that twist and sway,
In nature's arms, they drift away.

With every sigh, they weave their lore,
A tale of life, forevermore.
In the midnight hour, hearts do beat,
In sacred rhythm, soft and sweet.

Spirits swirl 'neath the starlit sky,
Their dance enchants, a gentle sigh.
In the twilight's embrace, they spin,
A timeless tale that draws us in.

Requiem for the Enchanted Traveler

Beneath the stars, a journey starts,
With restless feet and longing hearts.
The road ahead, a winding maze,
Lost in dreams, we drift in a haze.

Every step a memory made,
Paths of gold in the twilight fade.
Through realms where magic softly breathes,
In whispers lost among the leaves.

The traveler seeks what cannot be found,
In enchanted lands where spirits abound.
Once filled with hope, now drifting slow,
The echoes of laughter, a distant glow.

Through shadows deep, they wander far,
Chasing the light of a distant star.
Yet in the silence, a heartbeats sigh,
A requiem sung to the lost goodbye.

Memories linger, softly entwined,
In the fabric of time, love defined.
A gentle breeze whispers the tale,
Of a soul set free, destined to sail.

Phantoms in the Misty Grove

In the grove where shadows play,
Phantoms dance at end of day.
Mist enfolds like a whisper's breath,
Each wisp a flutter, hinting death.

Glimmers seen through fog so thick,
A fleeting glimpse, a magic trick.
Silent echoes of laughter ring,
In the stillness, the spirits sing.

Beneath the boughs of ancient trees,
They drift like leaves upon the breeze.
A tapestry woven of night and day,
In the folds of shadow, they play.

Secrets hidden in the gloom,
Where hope and fear together loom.
In every sigh, a story spun,
The dance of phantoms, never done.

As twilight falls, their forms appear,
A gathering of the lost and dear.
With every heartbeat, they linger near,
In the misty grove, no need for fear.

The Enchantment of Time Standstill

In moments lost, we find reprieve,
A pause in life that we believe.
Time trickles down like grains of sand,
A fleeting wish, a gentle hand.

In twilight's glow, the world stands still,
A breath held tight, time bends to will.
Each second swells, a treasure rare,
In the hush of night, we linger there.

The heartbeats echo, softly hum,
Inviting silence, the magic comes.
Caught between what was and dream,
In this stillness, the stars might gleam.

Memories swirl, a dance of fate,
In this embrace, we contemplate.
With every whisper, life reveals,
The enchantment that serendipity feels.

In this cocoon, we rise and fall,
A timeless realm that holds us all.
With every heartbeat, we find our thrill,
In the enchantment of time, we feel.

Haunting Riddles on Illusory Tracks

In the shadows whispers dwell,
Secrets wrapped in a silver shell.
Footsteps trace a hidden path,
Chasing silence, evading wrath.

Veils of night, the truth unfolds,
Stories wrapped in riddles old.
Each turn holds a mystery tight,
Guiding souls lost in the night.

A flicker of light, a fleeting glance,
Tempting hearts into the dance.
Illusions spin, softly weave,
What is real? What to believe?

Echoes stir from long ago,
Glimmers of life in the shadows know.
Each heartbeat, a thread in the weave,
A journey bound to deceive.

In this maze where whispers lure,
Mysteries linger, ripe and pure.
Find the key beneath the stone,
Only then will you atone.

The Sorcerer's Journey Through Night's End

On the horizon, stars collide,
The sorcerer rides, the night is wide.
Magic swirls in a silver mist,
Casting spells, impossible to resist.

With every breath, a whisper calls,
Through shadowed forests, by moonlit halls.
Steps of a wanderer, firm yet frail,
In the heart of darkness, he shall prevail.

Constellations weave a tale of old,
Of souls ablaze with dreams untold.
Chanting the names of ancient lore,
He awakens shadows, opens the door.

The path stretches long, the end unseen,
In the realm between where hopes convene.
Guided by dreams, he seeks the dawn,
A sorcerer's quest, till the light is drawn.

With every spell, he shapes his fate,
Embracing the night, challenging hate.
At night's end, visions align,
To rise with the sun, forever to shine.

Echoes of Dreams at the Crossroads

Where paths converge, old dreams sigh,
In the silence, wishes fly.
Whispers linger on the breeze,
Tales of heartache and moments seized.

Choices made, regrets unfold,
In the moonlight, stories told.
Every step, a chance we take,
Seeker's fate, awake or break.

In twilight shadows, truths arise,
Painted hopes adorn the skies.
At the junction, a solemn creed,
What we sow is what we need.

Echoes bounce off ancient stones,
Finding solace in whispered tones.
In every heartbeat, paths define,
A tapestry of dreams entwined.

Fate is forged in the silent night,
Under stars that burn so bright.
With open hearts, we bravely choose,
In this dance, we cannot lose.

Constellations of Wandering Wishes

Beneath the sky, where starlight plays,
Wishes scattered in cosmic arrays.
Each flicker holds a promise true,
In the darkness, dreams break through.

Galaxies spin, a dance of fate,
Mapping desires that love creates.
The heart drifts, a ship at sea,
Guided by hope, forever free.

In whispers soft, secrets unveil,
Silent journeys, a destined trail.
Through nebulas, the spirits soar,
In shimmering realms forevermore.

Tides of stars, a canvas vast,
Echoing wishes of the past.
In the night's embrace, dreams take flight,
Illuminating the darkest night.

So drift along, let your heart sing,
Follow the path that starlight brings.
In every glimpse, a wish ignites,
Constellations of enchanting nights.

Secrets Hidden by the Ancient Stone

Beneath the moss, a tale is spun,
Whispers of time, the ages run.
Silent watches, the stone guards tight,
Memories linger, lost from sight.

Ghostly shadows in twilight sway,
Holding secrets, night and day.
Fingers trace the weathered lines,
Pathways leading to ancient signs.

Each step echoes through the past,
Stories forgotten, shadows cast.
The heart beats slow, the air grows still,
Awakening dreams, a timeless thrill.

Eyes may search, but few will find,
The wisdom locked in the entwined.
Time stands guard with watchful stare,
In the stillness, answers bear.

Listen closely, for they will call,
The ancient whispers, past's enthrall.
Beneath the stone, the truth unfolds,
In hidden scripts, the tale is told.

The Dance of Echoing Dreams

In twilight glows, the shadows play,
Dreams awaken, drifting away.
Softly hums the breezy night,
Echoes dance in silver light.

Waves of stars on velvet flow,
Carrying whispers from below.
The moonlight weaves a timeless song,
As wandering spirits drift along.

Each heartbeat joins the cosmic sway,
With every breath, the night holds sway.
Visions sparkle, like fireflies,
In the quiet, where magic lies.

Threads of hope and past entwined,
Mystical pathways intertwined.
The dance unfolds in hazy dreams,
Life is more than what it seems.

So lose yourself in the gentle breeze,
Where echoing dreams find their ease.
In the silence, every heart sings,
The magic of night's hidden wings.

In the Wake of Wandering Spirits

On midnight trails where shadows roam,
Whispers guide the lost back home.
Footsteps linger, soft and slow,
As echoes tell where memories flow.

Flickering lights in distant trees,
Watch the dance carried by the breeze.
Specters linger like fragrant blooms,
In the silence, acceptance looms.

Haunting tales in the soft moon's glow,
Speak of journeys we may never know.
Guided hearts find strength in grace,
Within the wake, a cherished place.

Each spirit wanders, seeking peace,
In the soft hush, worries cease.
The path unwinds, the night feels warm,
Embracing remnants of the storm.

For every sigh upon the air,
Hints of stories wait to share.
In the hush of the night, we find,
The wandering spirits leave behind.

Veils of Enchantment in Twilight Shadows

Veils entwined in twilight's hand,
Mystic whispers in golden sand.
Secrets wrapped in shadows cast,
A dance of echoes, binding past.

The moonlight spills in silver streams,
Holding softly our secret dreams.
Every rustle, every sigh,
Weaves a tapestry in the sky.

Glimmers of hope in dusky skies,
Enchanting all with silent cries.
Hidden magic, pathways play,
In twilight moments, night meets day.

Ephemeral moments brush our skin,
Together breathe where love begins.
Through veils of night, the spirits lead,
In twilight's heart, we're all intrigued.

So linger here, where dreams entwine,
In shadows deep, our souls align.
In the stillness, enchantments flow,
In twilight shadows, love will grow.

Mysteries Beneath the Twilight Path

In shadows deep where whispers play,
The twilight path beckons astray.
Once known to few, now lost in time,
Its secrets weave a haunting rhyme.

A flicker here, a sighing breeze,
Tales of old beneath the trees.
Footsteps soft on ancient stone,
Echoes call in dusk alone.

Beneath the stars where dreams collide,
Nature's heart and fate's great tide.
Each twist and turn holds kin and lore,
Forever yearning, craving more.

A lantern's glow, a fleeting glance,
The path invites a secret dance.
With every step, a story dies,
Yet in the mist, a new one lies.

Embrace the night, let shadows weave,
In mystery's heart, take a breath, believe.
The twilight path, a journey vast,
Where future echoes linger past.

Lullabies of the Forgotten Wizards

In dim-lit rooms where shadows bend,
Ancient wizards' songs ascend.
Lullabies soft, with echoes wide,
A magic world where dreams abide.

Remembered words on parchment frayed,
Whispers of spells that night conveyed.
They drift like mist through hidden halls,
Each note a spark where silence calls.

Crystals hum with a gentle light,
Guiding seekers through the night.
Lost in time, yet close at hand,
The lullabies weave through the land.

Every gesture, flick of a wrist,
Conjures visions you can't resist.
A tale unfolds in hushed refrain,
Of wisdom deep and joy and pain.

Sleep now, dear child, as shadows grow,
Wizards' dreams in twilight flow.
Their lullabies cradle the air,
With each sweet note, take you there.

The Train that Crossed the Celestial Veil

Upon the tracks of stardust bright,
The train speeds forth through endless night.
Its whistle calls to the waiting soul,
As planets spin, the cosmos whole.

Through winding arcs of light and dark,
Each station holds a whispered spark.
With every stop, a story thrives,
Of shimmering dreams where magic dives.

Galaxies clash in a cosmic dance,
Passengers lost in a fleeting trance.
Time dissolves in the twilight glow,
As journeys beckon through realms unknown.

A glimpse of worlds beyond the skies,
Where hope and wonder always rise.
The train rolls on, through time and space,
With hearts that seek the stars' embrace.

As dawn approaches, the journey's end,
Yet in our hearts, the dreams extend.
The train that crossed the veil above,
Leaves trails of light, of hope and love.

Secrets of a Scattered Constellation

Amidst the stars where stories glow,
A scattered constellation's flow.
Each flicker holds a whispered truth,
A memory of long-lost youth.

In patterns drawn by cosmic hands,
Secrets linger in far-off lands.
They murmur softly through the night,
Guiding dreamers toward the light.

The nights unfold like tales unspooled,
Where wishes dance and hearts are fooled.
Each star a flicker, a spark of fate,
Binding souls in love's debate.

Together drifting, hearts aligned,
Chasing echoes of the divine.
In silence deep, their lore is spun,
A scattered dream, yet all as one.

So gaze upon that distant sky,
And listen close as night drifts by.
The secrets whispered by the stars,
Are echoes of our journey's scars.

Ghosts of the Sorcerer's Express

Whispers float on midnight air,
Shadows weave without a care,
Silhouettes upon the train,
Echoes of a long-lost chain.

Candles flicker, lanterns sway,
Souls that dance, then drift away,
Fragments of enchanted tales,
Riding on the spectral rails.

A ticket forged in ancient lore,
Destined to unlock a door,
Glistening runes, they softly glow,
Revealing paths where few may go.

Passengers in dreams entwined,
Seeking what they left behind,
Chimeras through the window pass,
Fleeting moments, echoes vast.

The sorcerer's charm won't let you rest,
A journey where the lost are blessed,
In twilight's grasp, time bends and sways,
On the express that never stays.

Twilight Secrets of the Mystical Route

In twilight's grasp, the secrets bloom,
Paths that trace the edge of gloom,
Whispers ride the evening breeze,
Holding tales of ancient keys.

Flickering lights on cobblestone,
Hidden worlds, so overgrown,
Every shadow, every spark,
Reveals the magic in the dark.

Beneath the arch, a portal gleams,
Flowing softly like distant dreams,
Winding round through time and space,
Where illusion starts to embrace.

Echoed footsteps, laughter near,
Lingering warmth, a touch sincere,
Veils of mystery, softly sway,
Leading wanderers astray.

The mystical route calls your name,
A journey stitched with hope and flame,
In twilight's fold, everything's true,
Secrets awaken, just for you.

Cracks in the Veil of Illusions

Listen close to the silent breaks,
Where the thin veneer often shakes,
Cracks that run like whispered thought,
Through illusions that fate has wrought.

When shadows stretch beneath the moon,
An unseen truth begins its tune,
Tides of magic ripple wide,
For those who dare, and cast aside.

Fractured light through a prism's gleam,
Teases forth a waking dream,
Through the seams, the light peeks clear,
Ghosts of knowledge linger near.

A flicker here, a shimmer there,
Shifting what lies everywhere,
Moments caught, too frail to hold,
Stories whispered, tales retold.

Where the veil gets thin at dusk,
Find the truth beneath the rust,
In cracks, the world begins to quiver,
Revealing lines that never shiver.

The Lament of Lost Spells

In the dark, the whispers rise,
Murmuros of ancient skies,
Chants forgotten, lost in time,
Echoing a distant rhyme.

Potions brewed with hands of fate,
To mend the heart, or change the state,
A flick of wand, a whispered plea,
Yet magic fades, leaves none to see.

Beneath the moon, the shadows dance,
Hoping still for one last chance,
To bind the moments held too tight,
To summon forth the vanished light.

Each incantation, soft and slow,
A glimpse of what could never grow,
Fleeting visions, frail and pale,
Sing together the lost spell's wail.

For in the silence, secrets dwell,
A bittersweet, melodic swell,
Echoes of a dream long passed,
The lament of spells, forever cast.

Echoes of Forgotten Magic

In shadows deep, the secrets lie,
A whispered spell, a lullaby.
The ancient trees, they sway and bend,
Guardians of time, forever friend.

Through twilight mist, the echoes call,
A dance of fireflies, a radiant sprawl.
Each flicker holds a tale untold,
Of magic lost, and dreams of gold.

The moonlit glade, a sacred place,
With every heartbeat, a soft embrace.
The stars align, their wishes spun,
Awakening hopes, with the morning sun.

In crystal streams, reflections gleam,
Mirroring wishes, a gentle dream.
The past remembers, the future waits,
In unity, love patiently creates.

Whispers Beneath the Winding Tracks

The trains hum softly, stories weave,
Through tunnels dark, where hearts believe.
Old wooden boards, they creak and sigh,
Holding secrets as they pass by.

Beneath the stars, the journey flows,
Through hidden paths, where no one knows.
Each station brings a fleeting glance,
Of lives entwined in fate's own dance.

In gentle winds, the echoes trace,
A tapestry of time and space.
With every mile, the memories bloom,
In whispered winds, they find their room.

The rusting steel, the fading light,
Tell tales of dreams that took to flight.
In every shadow, a story waits,
Beneath the tracks, love resonates.

Reveries of the Aether's Path

A silver thread through realms unseen,
Guides the dreamers where they convene.
With every breath, a wish takes flight,
In realms of dawn, beyond the night.

The skies unfold, in colors bright,
Painting hopes with the softest light.
In gentle whispers, the stars align,
A cosmic dance, a gift divine.

Upon the winds, the visions soar,
In harmony, the spirits roar.
Through endless skies, on wings of faith,
A journey bound, no time can waste.

With open hearts, the dreamers roam,
In every star, they find a home.
Together strong, through realms they glide,
In unity, forever side by side.

Fractured Dreams of Arcane Journeys

Fragments scattered, a puzzle vast,
Echoes whisper of a forgotten past.
Mystic pathways veiled in night,
Lead the way to joy and fright.

In candlelight, the shadows play,
Revealing truths that drift away.
With every sigh, a spell is cast,
Binding memories that long have passed.

Through velvet depths, the visions break,
A tapestry of dreams we make.
The moon will guide, the stars will lead,
In every heart, a silent need.

Tempting fate, we dance on edges,
Whispered promises, ancient pledges.
The journey winds, through time and space,
In fractured dreams, we find our place.

Remnants of Forgotten Incantations

In shadows deep where whispers weave,
Old spells linger, yet few believe.
The air thick with magic long lost,
We seek the echoes, count the cost.

Beneath the moon, in silence we tread,
Ancient runes, the words unsaid.
A flicker of light, a shiver of sound,
In the depths of night, their power is found.

Time unveils the secrets of old,
Stories of sorcery, waiting to unfold.
With each incantation softly sighed,
The remnants awaken, no longer denied.

Entwined in the past, they quietly wait,
For hearts open wide, to contemplate.
The rituals whispered, now dance on the breeze,
Calling the dreamers, with hearts at ease.

In the twilight's embrace, we gather near,
Awash in the magic, dispelling our fear.
For in those remnants, a promise lies,
Of forgotten realms, where true power flies.

The Veiled Journey of Wandering Souls

Through veils of mist, we wander alone,
Seeking the paths that time has grown.
Ghostly whispers, a soft lament,
In every heartbeat, our lives are spent.

The stars above, like eyes that observe,
Watch as our spirits twist and swerve.
Each step we take, a dance with the night,
Guided by hopes and flickers of light.

In shadows dark, we find our grace,
Ebbing and flowing, we trace the space.
With every sigh, the world feels wide,
In the veiled journey, our souls confide.

Fragments of memories lost in the flow,
Connections forged in the afterglow.
For every wanderer has a tale to tell,
Of how they wandered, and how they fell.

Though unclear our fate, we embrace the quest,
In the dance of the lost, we find our rest.
As souls intertwine, truly we find,
The veiled journey uniting all mankind.

Lament of the Wandering Sorcerer

A staff in hand, the world unwound,
In search of magic, yet silence found.
Wandering paths where shadows creep,
Dreams echo softly, but secrets keep.

With every spell, a story fades,
The once bright visions dim in the shades.
A longing heart, a whisper of pain,
In the sorcerer's tears, a loss to regain.

Among the stars, he casts his eyes,
Seeking the light in darkened skies.
Each incantation, a fragile thread,
Binding his past to the dreams now dead.

But the winds do carry his longing song,
In the twilight hours where shadows belong.
The wanderer moves, though weary and thin,
Searching the realms of the lost within.

In the quiet moments, he finds his peace,
For the wandering sorcerer never will cease.
In every lament, a glimmer of hope,
A spark of magic that helps him cope.

Time's Elusive Prism

Caught in a web of dreams divine,
Moments flicker, slip through time.
A prism of hues, reflecting the past,
Echoes of laughter, and shadows cast.

Each second a gem, dropped in the years,
Tales of joy and memories of tears.
In chambers of time, we dance and play,
Gathering fragments of yesterday.

An hourglass turns, yet we remain,
Sifting through grains of loss and gain.
With every heartbeat, we strive to see,
Life's vivid tapestry, wild and free.

In the twilight glow, we pause and gaze,
At the threads of fate in the sun's soft rays.
For time is both a thief and a gift,
In its elusive dance, our spirits lift.

So here we stand, at the edge of now,
Time's prism glimmers, and we take a bow.
Embrace the moment, let the past go,
In the present's light, our hearts will grow.

The Lure of Unwritten Spells

In shadows deep, the whispers call,
A breath of charm before the fall.
Ink on parchment waits for fate,
To weave the dreams we dare create.

Silent phrases softly glow,
In twilight's grasp, where wishes flow.
Each word a key to realms untold,
Unlocking wonders, bright and bold.

The air is thick with ancient lore,
A dance that legends can't ignore.
With every thought, a world takes flight,
As hopes ignite the starry night.

But fleeting time can dim the spark,
A fleeting glimpse that leaves a mark.
Yet still we yearn, our hearts compel,
To chase the lure of unwritten spells.

So gather close, all who believe,
In magic's touch, we shall achieve.
For when the ink begins to flow,
The stories of our lives will grow.

Whirlwinds of Magic and Memory

In swirling winds, the past appears,
With echoes sweet that draw us near.
Where laughter dances in the air,
And memories hold an endless flair.

The petals fall like drifting dreams,
In vibrant hues, they burst at seams.
Magic whispers through the trees,
Singing songs carried by the breeze.

Each moment etched, a cherished glow,
In hearts entwined, our spirits flow.
Together we brave the storms of fate,
As bonds grow strong, we navigate.

Through every twist of time we steer,
In whirlwinds wild, we conquer fear.
With every breath, the magic swells,
Forever bound by tales that tell.

So hold on tight to fleeting dreams,
Embrace the flow of life's wild streams.
For in the dance of time and space,
We find the spark that we all chase.

Fates Entwined in the Twilight's Embrace

As twilight wraps the world in gold,
Two fates converge, their hearts unfold.
In whispered sighs, the night descends,
Embracing souls that time transcends.

Stars ignite in the dusky skies,
Reflecting dreams within our eyes.
Each heartbeat synchronizes the song,
A melody where we belong.

The shadows linger, softly dance,
While secret glances spark romance.
With every touch, a story grows,
In twilight's arms, the magic flows.

As night unfolds its velvet deep,
We weave the dreams we dare to keep.
Fates entwined, we find our place,
In twilight's hush, we share a trace.

So let the stars guide us tonight,
As hope ignites, our hearts take flight.
With every moment, love we chase,
In the embrace of time's soft grace.

The Haunting of the Mystic Railway

In shadows cast by moonlit glow,
The whispers ride where no winds blow.
Tracks of steel through forests roam,
Echoes call from their ancient home.

Steam and smoke in hazy night,
Phantom trains in ghostly flight.
Flickering lights, a chilling breeze,
Carry tales from forgotten trees.

Laughter fades into the dark,
Hearts once brave, now just a spark.
Each curve hides a legend's tale,
Lost in mist, the old train wails.

Railway bends 'neath silver skies,
Where shadows dance and silence sighs.
One last ride, it beckons near,
Mystic calls that draw us here.

The journey ends, yet still it climbs,
Through haunted thoughts and timeless rhymes.
Onward still, the spirits play,
Bound forever, the mystic railway.

Lyrical Waters of Enchanted Streams

In the heart of the whispering woods,
Lies a stream where magic broods.
Glimmers dance on the surface bright,
Claiming dreams under the moonlight.

Ripples sing of forgotten lore,
Tales of love on an ancient shore.
Petals fall like notes in tune,
Softly rocking beneath the moon.

Waves that kiss the willow's edge,
Gently weave a silken pledge.
Songs that ripple, wild and free,
Flow like stories, endlessly.

Reflections weave in twilight's gaze,
Casting shadows, a real-time maze.
Beneath the arches of leafy trees,
The river hums a lullaby breeze.

Forever dancing, the waters gleam,
Holding secrets, a timeless dream.
In every drop, a world anew,
Enchanted streams weave magic's hue.

A Journey through Twilight's Veil

When dusk descends on the quiet glen,
Mysteries wake, their tales begin.
Softly woven in twilight's thread,
Whispers linger where shadows tread.

Footsteps hush on the gravel path,
Guided by a gentle aftermath.
Starlight shines through the fading day,
Leading hearts in a boundless sway.

Fog drifts low, a gossamer shroud,
Hiding wonders behind the crowd.
Crisp air wraps 'round each wistful sigh,
As time flows like clouds in the sky.

Voices echo through the misty night,
Heralding secrets in soft twilight.
Every bend reveals what's concealed,
New horizons glide unrevealed.

Eager souls seek the veils to part,
Finding beauty inside the heart.
Through twilight's whispers, we take flight,
Embarking on dreams like stars igniting.

The Sigh of Forgotten Sorcery

In ancient woods where shadows breathe,
Lies a secret none would believe.
Faded spells on the crumbling stone,
Echoes linger of the unknown.

Whispers crawl through the twisted vines,
Tales of magic lost in the pines.
With every sigh, the breeze complies,
Carrying wishes from the wise.

Moonlit glades hum with a soft tune,
Veiling dreams that dance with the moon.
Forgotten sorcery drifts on air,
Inviting those who dare to care.

Wands of willow and crystals bright,
Summon powers hidden from sight.
Bound by fate, they swirl and sway,
In enchanted realms where shadows play.

Figures fade, yet lore remains,
Tracing paths through ancient veins.
In the sighs of spells long lost,
The heart of magic shall count the cost.

Through these woods, the past aligns,
Binding the threads of forgotten times.
In every sigh, the world can see,
The pulse of sorcery, wild and free.